EMMANUEL JOSEPH

The Decision Loop, Creativity, Compassion, and the Path to Meaningful Connections

Copyright © 2025 by Emmanuel Joseph

All rights reserved. No part of this publication may be reproduced, stored or transmitted in any form or by any means, electronic, mechanical, photocopying, recording, scanning, or otherwise without written permission from the publisher. It is illegal to copy this book, post it to a website, or distribute it by any other means without permission.

First edition

This book was professionally typeset on Reedsy.
Find out more at reedsy.com

Contents

1   Chapter 1: The Genesis of the Decision Loop   1
2   Chapter 2: Embracing Uncertainty   3
3   Chapter 3: The Art of Mindful Decision-Making   5
4   Chapter 4: Navigating Ethical Dilemmas   7
5   Chapter 5: The Power of Resilience   9
6   Chapter 6: The Art of Letting Go   11
7   Chapter 7: The Dance of Intuition and Logic   13
8   Chapter 8: The Power of Reflection   15
9   Chapter 9: The Strength of Vulnerability   17
10   Chapter 10: The Essence of Gratitude   19
11   Chapter 11: The Journey of Self-Discovery   21
12   Chapter 12: The Practice of Presence   23
13   Chapter 13: The Strength of Boundaries   25
14   Chapter 14: The Dance of Freedom and Responsibility   27
15   Chapter 15: The Power of Forgiveness   29
16   Chapter 16: The Strength of Empathy   31
17   Chapter 17: The Journey Continues   33

1

Chapter 1: The Genesis of the Decision Loop

In the ever-evolving tapestry of human life, decisions form the intricate threads that bind experiences together. From the simplest of choices to the most complex dilemmas, the process of decision-making influences the course of our lives. The decision loop, a conceptual framework, unveils the patterns and principles that govern our choices. At its core lies the interplay between creativity, compassion, and the pursuit of meaningful connections. By understanding this loop, we can harness its power to navigate the labyrinth of life's uncertainties with grace and wisdom.

Creativity, the spark that ignites innovation, plays a pivotal role in the decision loop. It empowers individuals to envision possibilities beyond the conventional, to think outside the box, and to forge paths uncharted. When faced with a decision, creativity invites us to explore multiple perspectives, to challenge assumptions, and to embrace the unknown with curiosity and courage. Through creative thinking, we uncover novel solutions and unlock the potential for transformative outcomes.

Compassion, the gentle force that binds us to one another, is the heart of the decision loop. It calls us to consider the impact of our choices on others, to empathize with their experiences, and to act with kindness and understanding. Compassionate decision-making fosters connections rooted in trust and mutual respect. It reminds us that our actions ripple through the lives of those around us, shaping the collective fabric of our communities. By infusing our choices with compassion, we create a more harmonious and inclusive world.

The path to meaningful connections, the ultimate destination of the decision loop, is paved with intentionality and purpose. It is a journey that transcends the superficial and delves into the depths of authentic relationships. Meaningful connections are born from the synergy of creativity and compassion, where individuals unite in shared aspirations and mutual support. They are the lifeblood of a fulfilling existence, enriching our lives with a sense of belonging, purpose, and joy. Through the decision loop, we uncover the keys to nurturing these connections and weaving a tapestry of meaningful interactions.

2

Chapter 2: Embracing Uncertainty

Life is an intricate dance with uncertainty, where the only constant is change. The decision loop provides a roadmap for navigating this ever-shifting landscape, guiding us to embrace the unknown with resilience and grace. At the heart of this journey lies the recognition that uncertainty is not a foe to be vanquished but a companion to be embraced. By accepting the fluid nature of existence, we open ourselves to the boundless possibilities that lie beyond the horizon.

Creativity thrives in the fertile ground of uncertainty. It beckons us to explore uncharted territories, to venture into the realms of imagination and innovation. In the face of ambiguity, creative thinkers summon the courage to experiment, to take risks, and to reimagine what is possible. They understand that the seeds of brilliance are often sown in the soil of uncertainty, where the familiar gives way to the extraordinary. By embracing uncertainty, we unlock the potential for creative breakthroughs that redefine our reality.

Compassion provides a steady anchor in the turbulent seas of uncertainty. It reminds us that, despite the unpredictability of life, we are not alone. Compassionate decision-making fosters a sense of solidarity and support, encouraging us to extend a helping hand to those navigating their own uncertainties. It calls us to listen with empathy, to offer reassurance, and to act with kindness. In times of uncertainty, compassion becomes a beacon of hope, illuminating the path forward with the light of human connection.

THE DECISION LOOP, CREATIVITY, COMPASSION, AND THE PATH TO MEANINGFUL CONNECTIONS

Meaningful connections, the guiding stars in the night sky of uncertainty, are cultivated through intentionality and presence. They remind us that, amid the chaos, there is a profound beauty in shared experiences and authentic relationships. By nurturing these connections, we find solace and strength in the company of others. The decision loop teaches us that, in the face of uncertainty, the bonds we forge with others become our most valuable compass, guiding us toward a future brimming with possibility.

3

Chapter 3: The Art of Mindful Decision-Making

In the symphony of life, decisions are the notes that compose our unique melody. The decision loop invites us to approach decision-making with mindfulness and intentionality, to become conscious composers of our own fate. Mindful decision-making is an art that requires us to be present, to listen to the whispers of our intuition, and to honor the values that guide our journey.

Creativity infuses the process of mindful decision-making with vibrancy and depth. It encourages us to explore alternative perspectives, to engage in imaginative problem-solving, and to envision the ripple effects of our choices. Through creative thinking, we discover innovative solutions that align with our deepest aspirations. Mindfulness, in turn, grounds this creativity in the present moment, allowing us to make choices that are both inspired and aligned with our core values.

Compassion is the heart of mindful decision-making, inviting us to consider the well-being of ourselves and others in our choices. It calls us to approach decision-making with empathy, to weigh the impact of our actions on the greater good, and to act with kindness and integrity. By infusing our decisions with compassion, we create a ripple effect of positive change that extends far beyond our individual lives. Mindful decision-making, guided by compassion, becomes a powerful tool for fostering meaningful connections and creating a more just and inclusive world.

The path to meaningful connections, illuminated by mindful decision-making, is paved with authenticity and intention. Meaningful connections are born from choices that honor our true selves and reflect our deepest values. They are nurtured through acts of presence, vulnerability, and genuine care. The decision loop teaches us that, by making mindful choices, we cultivate relationships that are rich in meaning and purpose. These connections become the foundation of a fulfilling life, grounding us in a sense of belonging and interconnectedness.

4

Chapter 4: Navigating Ethical Dilemmas

Life presents us with ethical dilemmas that challenge our values and test our resolve. The decision loop provides a framework for navigating these moral crossroads with integrity and wisdom. At the heart of this journey lies the recognition that ethical decision-making is a nuanced and complex process, one that requires us to balance competing interests and consider the broader implications of our choices.

Creativity plays a vital role in navigating ethical dilemmas, offering innovative ways to address moral challenges. It encourages us to think beyond black-and-white solutions, to explore alternative perspectives, and to engage in creative problem-solving. By harnessing the power of creativity, we uncover ethical solutions that honor our values and promote the greater good. Creative thinkers approach ethical dilemmas with an open mind and a willingness to reimagine what is possible, forging paths that align with their deepest principles.

Compassion is the compass that guides us through the fog of ethical decision-making. It calls us to consider the impact of our choices on others, to act with empathy and kindness, and to prioritize the well-being of all involved. Compassionate decision-making fosters a sense of moral responsibility and encourages us to act with integrity. It reminds us that our actions have far-reaching consequences, and that by choosing compassion, we contribute to a more just and compassionate world.

THE DECISION LOOP, CREATIVITY, COMPASSION, AND THE PATH TO MEANINGFUL CONNECTIONS

The path to meaningful connections, navigated through ethical decision-making, is one of mutual respect and trust. Meaningful connections are built on the foundation of shared values and ethical principles. They are nurtured through acts of integrity, honesty, and genuine care. The decision loop teaches us that, by making ethical choices, we cultivate relationships that are rooted in trust and authenticity. These connections become a source of strength and inspiration, guiding us toward a life of purpose and fulfillment.

5

Chapter 5: The Power of Resilience

Resilience is the strength that allows us to bounce back from adversity and continue moving forward. The decision loop teaches us that resilience is not just an innate quality but a skill that can be cultivated through intentional choices. At the heart of this journey lies the recognition that resilience is a dynamic process, one that requires us to adapt, persevere, and find meaning in the face of challenges.

Creativity is a powerful ally in building resilience. It invites us to see challenges as opportunities for growth and transformation, to think outside the box, and to reimagine what is possible. Creative thinkers approach adversity with a sense of curiosity and a willingness to explore new solutions. By harnessing the power of creativity, we find innovative ways to overcome obstacles and emerge stronger on the other side. Resilience, fueled by creativity, becomes a catalyst for personal and collective growth.

Compassion is the bedrock of resilience, providing a source of strength and support in times of difficulty. It calls us to extend kindness to ourselves and others, to offer empathy and understanding, and to act with care. Compassionate decision-making fosters a sense of solidarity and connection, reminding us that we are not alone in our struggles. By choosing compassion, we create a network of support that bolsters our resilience and helps us navigate the storms of life with grace.

The path to meaningful connections, illuminated by resilience, is one of mutual support and shared growth. Meaningful connections are forged through the bonds of shared experiences and the collective strength that arises from overcoming challenges together. They are nurtured through acts of presence, empathy, and genuine care. The decision loop teaches us that, by building resilience, we cultivate relationships that are rich in meaning and purpose. These connections become a source of inspiration and strength, guiding us toward a life of fulfillment and joy.

6

Chapter 6: The Art of Letting Go

In the journey of life, there are times when we must let go of what no longer serves us to make room for new possibilities. The decision loop teaches us that the art of letting go is a vital aspect of personal growth and transformation. At the heart of this journey lies the recognition that letting go is not an act of defeat but an act of liberation. By releasing what no longer aligns with our values and aspirations, we open ourselves to the boundless potential of the future.

Creativity plays a pivotal role in the art of letting go by encouraging us to envision new possibilities and to reimagine our future. It invites us to explore alternative paths, to embrace change with curiosity and courage, and to see the act of letting go as an opportunity for growth. Creative thinkers understand that letting go is not an end but a beginning, a chance to create something new and beautiful from the ashes of the past. By harnessing the power of creativity, we find the strength to let go and the vision to move forward.

Compassion is the gentle force that guides us through the process of letting go. It calls us to be kind to ourselves and others, to offer empathy and understanding, and to act with care. Compassionate decision-making fosters a sense of healing and renewal, reminding us that letting go is a natural part of the human experience. By choosing compassion, we create a space for new possibilities to emerge, allowing us to move forward with grace and dignity.

THE DECISION LOOP, CREATIVITY, COMPASSION, AND THE PATH TO MEANINGFUL CONNECTIONS

The path to meaningful connections, illuminated by the art of letting go, is one of renewal and transformation. Meaningful connections are nurtured through acts of presence, vulnerability, and genuine care. They remind us that, amid the cycles of change, there is a profound beauty in the bonds we share with others. The decision loop teaches us that, by letting go of what no longer serves us, we create space for new connections that are rich in meaning and purpose. These connections become a source of inspiration and strength, guiding us toward a life of fulfillment and joy.

7

Chapter 7: The Dance of Intuition and Logic

The decision loop reveals the delicate dance between intuition and logic, two powerful forces that guide our choices. At the heart of this journey lies the recognition that both intuition and logic are essential elements of decision-making, each offering unique insights and perspectives. By embracing the interplay between these forces, we can make more informed and balanced choices.

Creativity thrives in the space where intuition and logic intersect. It invites us to explore the boundaries of both realms, to harness the power of our imagination, and to engage in innovative problem-solving. Creative thinkers understand that intuition and logic are not opposing forces but complementary allies. By integrating intuition and logic, we unlock the potential for creative breakthroughs that redefine our reality.

Compassion serves as the bridge that connects intuition and logic, fostering a sense of harmony and balance. It calls us to approach decision-making with empathy, to consider the well-being of ourselves and others, and to act with kindness and integrity. Compassionate decision-making reminds us that our choices have far-reaching consequences, and that by choosing compassion, we create a ripple effect of positive change.

The path to meaningful connections, guided by the dance of intuition and logic, is one of balance and harmony. Meaningful connections are nurtured through acts of presence, vulnerability, and genuine care. They remind us that, amid the complexities of decision-making, there is a profound beauty in the bonds we share with others. The decision loop teaches us that, by integrating intuition and logic, we cultivate relationships that are rich in meaning and purpose. These connections become a source of inspiration and strength, guiding us toward a life of fulfillment and joy.

8

Chapter 8: The Power of Reflection

Reflection is the mirror that allows us to see ourselves more clearly, to understand our choices, and to learn from our experiences. The decision loop teaches us that reflection is a vital aspect of personal growth and transformation. At the heart of this journey lies the recognition that reflection is not just a passive activity but an active process of self-discovery and insight.

Creativity infuses the process of reflection with vibrancy and depth. It invites us to explore alternative perspectives, to engage in imaginative problem-solving, and to envision the ripple effects of our choices. Through creative thinking, we discover innovative solutions that align with our deepest aspirations. Reflection, in turn, grounds this creativity in the present moment, allowing us to make choices that are both inspired and aligned with our core values.

Compassion is the heart of reflection, inviting us to consider the well-being of ourselves and others in our choices. It calls us to approach reflection with empathy, to weigh the impact of our actions on the greater good, and to act with kindness and integrity. By infusing our reflections with compassion, we create a ripple effect of positive change that extends far beyond our individual lives. Reflection, guided by compassion, becomes a powerful tool for fostering meaningful connections and creating a more just and inclusive world.

The path to meaningful connections, illuminated by reflection, is paved with authenticity and intention. Meaningful connections are born from choices that honor our true selves and reflect our deepest values. They are nurtured through acts of presence, vulnerability, and genuine care. The decision loop teaches us that, by engaging in reflection, we cultivate relationships that are rich in meaning and purpose. These connections become the foundation of a fulfilling life, grounding us in a sense of belonging and interconnectedness.

9

Chapter 9: The Strength of Vulnerability

Vulnerability is the strength that allows us to be authentic and open, to share our true selves with others, and to forge deep and meaningful connections. The decision loop teaches us that vulnerability is not a weakness but a source of power and resilience. At the heart of this journey lies the recognition that vulnerability is the gateway to authenticity and connection.

Creativity thrives in the space of vulnerability, inviting us to explore the depths of our emotions, to engage in imaginative problem-solving, and to envision new possibilities. Creative thinkers understand that vulnerability is not an end but a beginning, a chance to create something new and beautiful from the depths of our experiences. By harnessing the power of creativity, we find the strength to be vulnerable and the vision to move forward.

Compassion is the gentle force that guides us through the process of vulnerability. It calls us to be kind to ourselves and others, to offer empathy and understanding, and to act with care. Compassionate decision-making fosters a sense of healing and renewal, reminding us that vulnerability is a natural part of the human experience. By choosing compassion, we create a space for new possibilities to emerge, allowing us to move forward with grace and dignity.

The path to meaningful connections, illuminated by vulnerability, is one of authenticity and depth. Meaningful connections are nurtured through acts of presence, vulnerability, and genuine care. They remind us that, amid the cycles of change, there is a profound beauty in the bonds we share with others. The decision loop teaches us that, by embracing vulnerability, we cultivate relationships that are rich in meaning and purpose. These connections become a source of inspiration and strength, guiding us toward a life of fulfillment and joy.

10

Chapter 10: The Essence of Gratitude

Gratitude is the lens that allows us to see the beauty in our lives, to appreciate the gifts we have been given, and to cultivate a sense of abundance. The decision loop teaches us that gratitude is not just an emotion but a practice, one that can transform our lives and our relationships. At the heart of this journey lies the recognition that gratitude is the key to a fulfilling and meaningful existence.

Creativity infuses the practice of gratitude with vibrancy and depth. It invites us to explore the many ways in which we can express our appreciation, to engage in imaginative acts of kindness, and to envision the ripple effects of our gratitude. Creative thinkers understand that gratitude is not just a feeling but a way of being, a chance to create something new and beautiful from the abundance of our lives. By harnessing the power of creativity, we find the strength to practice gratitude and the vision to move forward.

Compassion is the heart of gratitude, inviting us to consider the well-being of ourselves and others in our choices. It calls us to approach gratitude with empathy, to weigh the impact of our actions on the greater good, and to act with kindness and integrity. By infusing our gratitude with compassion, we create a ripple effect of positive change that extends far beyond our individual lives. Gratitude, guided by compassion, becomes a powerful tool for fostering meaningful connections and creating a more just and inclusive world.

The path to meaningful connections, illuminated by gratitude, is paved with authenticity and intention. Meaningful connections are born from choices that honor our true selves and reflect our deepest values. They are nurtured through acts of presence, vulnerability, and genuine care. The decision loop teaches us that, by practicing gratitude, we cultivate relationships that are rich in meaning and purpose. These connections become the foundation of a fulfilling life, grounding us in a sense of belonging and interconnectedness.

11

Chapter 11: The Journey of Self-Discovery

Self-discovery is the journey that allows us to understand ourselves more deeply, to uncover our true selves, and to live in alignment with our values. The decision loop teaches us that self-discovery is not a destination but a continuous process of growth and transformation. At the heart of this journey lies the recognition that self-discovery is the key to a fulfilling and meaningful existence.

Creativity infuses the journey of self-discovery with vibrancy and depth. It invites us to explore the many facets of our identity, to engage in imaginative acts of self-expression, and to envision the ripple effects of our choices. Creative thinkers understand that self-discovery is not just a feeling but a way of being, a chance to create something new and beautiful from the abundance of our lives. By harnessing the power of creativity, we find the strength to embark on the journey of self-discovery and the vision to move forward.

Compassion is the heart of self-discovery, inviting us to consider the well-being of ourselves and others in our choices. It calls us to approach self-discovery with empathy, to weigh the impact of our actions on the greater good, and to act with kindness and integrity. By infusing our self-discovery with compassion, we create a ripple effect of positive change that extends far beyond our individual lives. Self-discovery, guided by compassion, becomes a powerful tool for fostering meaningful connections and creating a more just and inclusive world.

The path to meaningful connections, illuminated by self-discovery, is paved with authenticity and intention. Meaning-discovery, we cultivate relationships that are rich in meaning and purpose. These connections become the foundation of a fulfilling life, grounding us in a sense of belonging and interconnectedness.

12

Chapter 12: The Practice of Presence

Presence is the art of being fully engaged in the present moment, to savor the richness of our experiences, and to connect deeply with ourselves and others. The decision loop teaches us that presence is not just a state of mind but a practice, one that can transform our lives and our relationships. At the heart of this journey lies the recognition that presence is the key to a fulfilling and meaningful existence.

Creativity infuses the practice of presence with vibrancy and depth. It invites us to explore the many ways in which we can be present, to engage in imaginative acts of mindfulness, and to envision the ripple effects of our presence. Creative thinkers understand that presence is not just a feeling but a way of being, a chance to create something new and beautiful from the abundance of our lives. By harnessing the power of creativity, we find the strength to practice presence and the vision to move forward.

Compassion is the heart of presence, inviting us to consider the well-being of ourselves and others in our choices. It calls us to approach presence with empathy, to weigh the impact of our actions on the greater good, and to act with kindness and integrity. By infusing our presence with compassion, we create a ripple effect of positive change that extends far beyond our individual lives. Presence, guided by compassion, becomes a powerful tool for fostering meaningful connections and creating a more just and inclusive world.

The path to meaningful connections, illuminated by presence, is paved with authenticity and intention. Meaningful connections are born from choices that honor our true selves and reflect our deepest values. They are nurtured through acts of presence, vulnerability, and genuine care. The decision loop teaches us that, by practicing presence, we cultivate relationships that are rich in meaning and purpose. These connections become the foundation of a fulfilling life, grounding us in a sense of belonging and interconnectedness.

13

Chapter 13: The Strength of Boundaries

Boundaries are the lines that define our personal space, our values, and our sense of self. The decision loop teaches us that boundaries are not barriers but essential elements of healthy relationships and self-care. At the heart of this journey lies the recognition that boundaries are the key to a fulfilling and meaningful existence.

Creativity infuses the practice of setting boundaries with vibrancy and depth. It invites us to explore the many ways in which we can define our personal space, to engage in imaginative acts of self-expression, and to envision the ripple effects of our boundaries. Creative thinkers understand that boundaries are not just lines but a chance to create something new and beautiful from the abundance of our lives. By harnessing the power of creativity, we find the strength to set boundaries and the vision to move forward.

Compassion is the heart of setting boundaries, inviting us to consider the well-being of ourselves and others in our choices. It calls us to approach boundaries with empathy, to weigh the impact of our actions on the greater good, and to act with kindness and integrity. By infusing our boundaries with compassion, we create a ripple effect of positive change that extends far beyond our individual lives. Boundaries, guided by compassion, become a powerful tool for fostering meaningful connections and creating a more just and inclusive world.

The path to meaningful connections, illuminated by boundaries, is paved with authenticity and intention. Meaningful connections are born from choices that honor our true selves and reflect our deepest values. They are nurtured through acts of presence, vulnerability, and genuine care. The decision loop teaches us that, by setting boundaries, we cultivate relationships that are rich in meaning and purpose. These connections become the foundation of a fulfilling life, grounding us in a sense of belonging and interconnectedness.

14

Chapter 14: The Dance of Freedom and Responsibility

The decision loop reveals the delicate dance between freedom and responsibility, two powerful forces that guide our choices. At the heart of this journey lies the recognition that both freedom and responsibility are essential elements of a fulfilling and meaningful existence. By embracing the interplay between these forces, we can make more informed and balanced choices.

Creativity thrives in the space where freedom and responsibility intersect. It invites us to explore the boundaries of both realms, to harness the power of our imagination, and to engage in innovative problem-solving. Creative thinkers understand that freedom and responsibility are not opposing forces but complementary allies. By integrating freedom and responsibility, we unlock the potential for creative breakthroughs that redefine our reality.

Compassion serves as the bridge that connects freedom and responsibility, fostering a sense of harmony and balance. It calls us to approach decision-making with empathy, to consider the well-being of ourselves and others, and to act with kindness and integrity. Compassionate decision-making reminds us that our choices have far-reaching consequences, and that by choosing compassion, we create a ripple effect of positive change.

The path to meaningful connections, guided by the dance of freedom and responsibility, is one of balance and harmony. Meaningful connections are nurtured through acts of presence, vulnerability, and genuine care. They remind us that, amid the complexities of decision-making, there is a profound beauty in the bonds we share with others. The decision loop teaches us that, by integrating freedom and responsibility, we cultivate relationships that are rich in meaning and purpose. These connections become a source of inspiration and strength, guiding us toward a life of fulfillment and joy.

15

Chapter 15: The Power of Forgiveness

Forgiveness is the strength that allows us to let go of past hurts, to heal from our wounds, and to move forward with grace and compassion. The decision loop teaches us that forgiveness is not just an act but a practice, one that can transform our lives and our relationships. At the heart of this journey lies the recognition that forgiveness is the key to a fulfilling and meaningful existence.

Creativity infuses the practice of forgiveness with vibrancy and depth. It invites us to explore the many ways in which we can let go of past hurts, to engage in imaginative acts of healing, and to envision the ripple effects of our forgiveness. Creative thinkers understand that forgiveness is not just a feeling but a way of being, a chance to create something new and beautiful from the abundance of our lives. By harnessing the power of creativity, we find the strength to forgive and the vision to move forward.

Compassion is the heart of forgiveness, inviting us to consider the well-being of ourselves and others in our choices. It calls us to approach forgiveness with empathy, to weigh the impact of our actions on the greater good, and to act with kindness and integrity. By infusing our forgiveness with compassion, we create a ripple effect of positive change that extends far beyond our individual lives. Forgiveness, guided by compassion, becomes a powerful tool for fostering meaningful connections and creating a more just and inclusive world.

THE DECISION LOOP, CREATIVITY, COMPASSION, AND THE PATH TO MEANINGFUL CONNECTIONS

The path to meaningful connections, illuminated by forgiveness, is paved with authenticity and intention. Meaningful connections are born from choices that honor our true selves and reflect our deepest values. They are nurtured through acts of presence, vulnerability, and genuine care. The decision loop teaches us that, by practicing forgiveness, we cultivate relationships that are rich in meaning and purpose. These connections become the foundation of a fulfilling life, grounding us in a sense of belonging and interconnectedness.

16

Chapter 16: The Strength of Empathy

Empathy is the strength that allows us to understand and share the feelings of others, to connect deeply with their experiences, and to act with compassion and kindness. The decision loop teaches us that empathy is not just an emotion but a practice, one that can transform our lives and our relationships. At the heart of this journey lies the recognition that empathy is the key to a fulfilling and meaningful existence.

Creativity infuses the practice of empathy with vibrancy and depth. It invites us to explore the many ways in which we can connect with others, to engage in imaginative acts of understanding, and to envision the ripple effects of our empathy. Creative thinkers understand that empathy is not just a feeling but a way of being, a chance to create something new and beautiful from the abundance of our lives. By harnessing the power of creativity, we find the strength to practice empathy and the vision to move forward.

Compassion is the heart of empathy, inviting us to consider the well-being of ourselves and others in our choices. It calls us to approach empathy with kindness, to weigh the impact of our actions on the greater good, and to act with integrity. By infusing our empathy with compassion, we create a ripple effect of positive change that extends far beyond our individual lives. Empathy, guided by compassion, becomes a powerful tool for fostering meaningful connections and creating a more just and inclusive world.

The path to meaningful connections, illuminated by empathy, is paved with authenticity and intention. Meaningful connections are born from choices that honor our true selves and reflect our deepest values. They are nurtured through acts of presence, vulnerability, and genuine care. The decision loop teaches us that, by practicing empathy, we cultivate relationships that are rich in meaning and purpose. These connections become the foundation of a fulfilling life, grounding us in a sense of belonging and interconnectedness.

17

Chapter 17: The Journey Continues

The decision loop is a continuous journey, one that invites us to explore the depths of our creativity, compassion, and connection. It teaches us that the path to a fulfilling and meaningful existence is not a destination but a process, one that requires us to be present, to be intentional, and to be compassionate. At the heart of this journey lies the recognition that our choices, guided by the decision loop, have the power to transform our lives and our relationships.

Creativity infuses the journey with vibrancy and depth. It invites us to explore the many ways in which we can create a fulfilling and meaningful existence, to engage in imaginative acts of self-expression, and to envision the ripple effects of our choices. Creative thinkers understand that the journey is not just a feeling but a way of being, a chance to create something new and beautiful from the abundance of our lives. By harnessing the power of creativity, we find the strength to embark on the journey and the vision to move forward.

Compassion is the heart of the journey, inviting us to consider the well-being of ourselves and others in our choices. It calls us to approach the journey with empathy, to weigh the impact of our actions on the greater good, and to act with kindness and integrity. By infusing our journey with compassion, we create a ripple effect of positive change that extends far beyond our individual lives. The journey, guided by compassion, becomes a powerful tool for fostering meaningful connections and creating a more just and inclusive world.

The path to meaningful connections, illuminated by the journey, is paved with authenticity and intention. Meaningful connections are born from choices that honor our true selves and reflect our deepest values. They are nurtured through acts of presence, vulnerability, and genuine care. The decision loop teaches us that, by embarking on the journey, we cultivate relationships that are rich in meaning and purpose. These connections become the foundation of a fulfilling life, grounding us in a sense of belonging and interconnectedness.

As the journey of life continues, the decision loop serves as a compass, guiding us through the intricate dance of creativity, compassion, and connection. It reminds us that our choices have the power to shape our reality and that, by embracing the decision loop, we can create a life of fulfillment and joy. The journey is not a destination but a continuous process of growth and transformation, one that invites us to be present, to be intentional, and to be compassionate. Through the decision loop, we discover the path to a meaningful and purposeful existence, one that is rich in creativity, compassion, and connection.

The decision loop is a powerful framework that reveals the patterns and principles guiding our choices. It teaches us that creativity, compassion, and connection are the keys to a fulfilling and meaningful existence. By embracing the decision loop, we can navigate the uncertainties of life with grace and wisdom, creating a life that is rich in meaning and purpose. The journey of life is a continuous process of growth and transformation, one that invites us to be present, to be intentional, and to be compassionate. Through the decision loop, we discover the path to a meaningful and purposeful existence, one that is rich in creativity, compassion, and connection. As we embark on this journey, we are reminded that our choices have the power to shape our reality and that, by embracing the decision loop, we can create a life of fulfillment and joy.

"**The Decision Loop: Creativity, Compassion, and the Path to Meaningful Connections**" is a transformative exploration of the interplay between creativity, compassion, and the pursuit of meaningful connections. This book delves into the decision loop, a conceptual framework that reveals the patterns and principles guiding our choices. Through seventeen insightful chapters, readers will embark on a journey of self-discovery, resilience, and intentionality, uncovering the keys to navigating life's uncertainties with grace and wisdom. Each chapter weaves together the themes of creativity, compassion, and connection, offering practical insights and inspiring stories that illuminate the path to a fulfilling and meaningful existence.

www.ingramcontent.com/pod-product-compliance
Lightning Source LLC
LaVergne TN
LVHW020458080526
838202LV00057B/6030